JUST DESSERTS

And Other Treats
for Kids to Make

Written by Marilyn Linton
Illustrated by Barbara Reid

KIDS CAN PRESS

To Charley

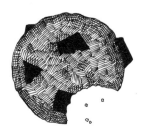

First U.S. edition 1998
Revised Canadian edition 1998

Published in Canada by
Kids Can Press Ltd.
29 Birch Avenue
Toronto, ON M4V 1E2

Published in the U.S. by
Kids Can Press Ltd.
85 River Rock Drive, Suite 202
Buffalo, NY 14207

Text copyright © 1986 by Marilyn Linton
Illustrations copyright © 1986, 1998 by Barbara Reid

Edited by Valerie Wyatt
Designed by Karen Powers
Cover Photos by Frank Baldassarra

Printed and bound in Canada

CMC 86 0 9 8 7 6 5 4 3 2

Canadian Cataloguing in Publication Data

Linton, Marilyn
Just desserts : a cookbook for kids

Includes index.

ISBN 0-921103-02-6

1. Desserts – Juvenile literature. I. Title.

TX773.L56 1986   641.8'6   C86-093765-8

CONTENTS

Acknowledgments

Many people helped in the preparation of this book. Some tasted, others tested. Some shared their recipes, others the sugar or flour from their pantries. Some loved what they tasted, others suggested improvements. Whatever your part, thank you to Barbara Pathy; Barb Holland; Marian Hebb; Doug, Sam and Tanya Linton; the kids at Deer Park School who helped; Laura Bennick; Michelle Heron; Terry Allen; Jenny, Vicki and Tim Pritchard; Franny Linton; The Great Book Group; Jessica Clarke; and Valerie, Ricky and Val from Kids Can Press.

The author also wishes to thank the following people: Jerry Ballon for peanut-butter candy cheesecake; Nettie Cronish for pistachio carrot cake; Sue Devor for cinnamon pear cake; Eleanor Schott for lemon angel pie; Katie Waverman for maple butter tarts; Lucy Waverman for fat alberts; and Hayley Wine for candy cookies.

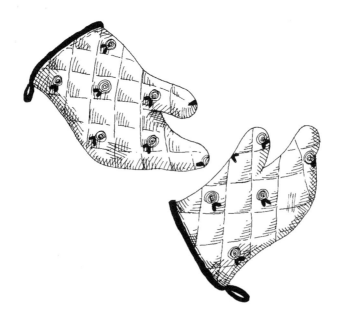

Introduction

You've probably been told to eat your vegetables. But chances are, no one has ever had to remind you to eat your dessert. This book is all about desserts — yummy cookies, dreamy pies, fruity shakes, chocolaty cakes and more. This book is also about cooking. You'll learn how to turn a strawberry into a shake, a chocolate bar into a cookie and tomato soup into a cake. And you'll discover how to pat pastry into a piecrust to make a fruit pizza, how to beat egg whites until they stand in stiff peaks for lemon angel pie and how to bake muffins until they're puffed and golden. When you're cooking, remember that adults love desserts, too. You'll want to share what you've made with family and friends.

Many of the recipes make wonderful breakfasts and tasty snacks. All of them can be enjoyed after dinner. So don't forget to eat your vegetables — whatever your age. Because then comes dessert!

Note: Before serving food to friends, it's always a good idea to ask them about any allergies they might have. Some of the recipes in this book include nuts or peanut butter, so before offering samples to friends or family, make sure that no one is allergic to nuts. (In some cases, the nuts can be left out of the recipe without affecting the result.)

Cooking words

BEAT
To make a mixture smooth by adding air with a fast whipping or stirring motion, using a spoon, whisk, eggbeater or electric mixer.

BLEND
To mix together two or more ingredients by hand or by electric blender.

BOIL
To heat any liquid on high heat until bubbles rise to its surface and break. The boiling temperature of water is 212 °F (100°C).

CHOP
To cut ingredients into small pieces with a knife.

CORE
To remove the core of fruit with a knife.

CREAM
To beat a mixture with a wooden spoon or an electric mixer until it is soft and smooth or light and fluffy.

DUST
To sprinkle flour in a greased baking pan so that a cake doesn't stick to the bottom. First, smear a spoonful of butter or margarine over the bottom and sides of the pan with a piece of waxed paper or paper towel. Then put a tablespoon (15 mL) of flour into the pan and shake it around so that some of the flour gets on the sides and bottom of the pan.

FOLD
To add ingredients gently to a mixture. A spatula works best for folding. Cut down through the mixture with the spatula, then across the bottom to the top. Repeat several times.

GARNISH
To decorate a finished dessert with small pieces of food.

GRATE
To make an ingredient, such as chocolate or the rind of an orange, into tiny pieces using a grater.

GREASE
To grease a pan or cookie sheet with butter or margarine so that the food doesn't stick to it when baking. Put a spoonful of butter or margarine on a piece of waxed paper or paper towel and smear it over the bottom of the cookie sheet or the sides and bottom of a baking pan. (Baking pans should then be dusted with flour.)

MELT

To heat ingredients such as chocolate and butter before adding them to other ingredients. To melt something, cook it in a small pan over very low heat so that it doesn't burn.

PEEL

To remove the skin or outer layer of a fruit using a knife.

PIT

To remove the seed from a fruit such as a cherry.

PUREE

To use a blender to turn a food such as fruit into a mixture as smooth as baby food.

SEPARATE

To separate an egg, use two bowls. Tap the side of the egg against the side of one bowl. Pull apart the top and bottom of the eggshell. Let the yellow yolk sit in half the eggshell and gently drip all of the egg white into one of the bowls. Slightly tip the shell holding the yolk in it to drip out as much of the white as you can. Then plop the egg yolk into the other bowl. Use the tip of your fingers to remove any broken pieces of shell from the yolk or the white. Make sure no yolk gets into your white or you won't be able to whip the egg whites.

SIFT

To pour one or more dry ingredients through a sieve or sifter to get air into the mixture and mix the ingredients together.

SIMMER

To cook any liquid mixture on medium-low heat so that the mixture cooks but bubbles do not form.

STIFF PEAKS

When egg whites are beaten, they will form peaks that stand up straight as the beaters are lifted out of the mixing bowl.

TOSS

To mix ingredients together lightly by lifting and dropping them with two forks or two spoons.

WHIP

To whip cream, use a mixer or eggbeater to mix the cream quickly. Air gets into the mixture, making it lighter and increasing its volume. Cream is whipped when peaks form. If you overwhip cream, though, you make butter!

WHISK

To combine ingredients together using a side-to-side motion with a wire whisk.

Utensils

BLENDER

An electric blender helps make drinks frothy and sauces smooth. When you need to use a blender for a recipe, ask an adult for help. Always start at low speed and keep the lid on while blending. Do not put your hands in the blender jar or remove the jar until the motor has stopped completely. If you don't have a blender, you can shake the ingredients together in a covered jar as long as you make sure you cut them up finely first.

COOKIE SHEETS

Most cookie recipes work best if you grease the cookie sheet by smearing on a thin layer of butter, margarine or shortening before placing the uncooked cookies on it. This prevents cookies from sticking during cooking. You can usually get by with one cookie sheet instead of two by removing cookies when they come out of the oven and putting on the new ones.

DOUBLE BOILER

In this set of two pots, water is put in the bottom, slightly larger pot, and the slightly smaller pot (which fits into the top of the larger one) contains the mixture you want to cook. Ingredients that burn easily (such as chocolate) or that need to be thickened evenly and slowly (such as custard) are best melted or cooked in a double boiler. When heating the water in the bottom pot, bring it to a simmer, not to a rolling boil.

EGGBEATER

Used to whip egg whites or egg yolks to make a mixture light and fluffy.

MUFFIN PANS

Use medium-sized muffin pans for the recipes in this book (the muffins at their widest part measure 7 cm/2¾ inches). Muffin pans should be greased or lined with paper muffin cups before being filled. Muffins bake more evenly if you leave one muffin cup empty and partially fill it with water.

SIEVE OR SIFTER

A wire mesh sieve or a sifter is necessary for sifting together dry ingredients.

SPATULA

A paddle-shaped metal, plastic or wood spatula is useful for lifting foods such as pancakes or cookies off a hot pan. (If your pan has a plastic coating on it, don't use a metal spatula or it will scratch.) A rubber spatula is also good for scraping foods from the side of a bowl or for folding in ingredients.

SPRINGFORM PAN

A round cake pan with a metal collar that can be unlocked and removed after the cake is baked and cooled.

Microwave tips

Many of the recipes in this book can be done partially or completely in a microwave oven. If you're using a microwave, be sure to use glass or special microwavable baking dishes. Here are some microwave tips for dessert making. Most only take a few seconds on high.

• Soften butter, cream cheese or peanut butter.

• Heat pies, cakes and other desserts before serving.

• Soften hard ice cream so that it's easier to scoop or spread.

• Thaw frozen desserts and muffins on low until defrosted.

• Heat fondues, hot drinks and hot sauces.

• Melt chocolate by putting it in a microwavable dish and heating it on medium for 2 minutes per 28 g (1 oz.).

The following power levels have been used in microwave recipes in this book:

high.	100% power
medium high . . .	70% power
medium	50% power
medium low. . . .	30% power
low	10% power

Measuring cups and spoons

Recipes work best if you use exact measurements. To do this, you need special cooking measuring cups and spoons. In this book, we've used two systems of cooking measures — imperial and metric. You can choose whichever system you wish, but once you've chosen, stick to it; don't switch between imperial and metric measures in a recipe. Here are the abbreviations used in this book:

IMPERIAL		**METRIC**	
c.	cup	mL	milliliter
tsp.	teaspoon	L	liter
tbsp.	tablespoon	g	gram
oz.	ounce	cm	centimeter
lb.	pound		

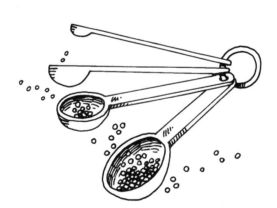

COOKIES

Chocolate chewies

Eat these chewy granola bars with yogurt, a piece of fruit and juice for a nice, light lunch.

YOU WILL NEED

125 mL	soft unsalted butter or margarine	½ c.
175 mL	brown sugar, lightly packed	¾ c.
1	egg	
5 mL	vanilla	1 tsp.
250 mL	all-purpose flour	1 c.
5 mL	baking soda	1 tsp.
	pinch of salt	
125 mL	granola cereal	½ c.
125 mL	sunflower seeds, shelled	½ c.
125 mL	semisweet chocolate chips	½ c.

UTENSILS

large bowl	wooden spoon
measuring cups	2.5 L (9 in.) square baking pan
measuring spoons	

1 Heat the oven to 375°F (190°C) and lightly grease the baking pan. In a large bowl, mix together the butter or margarine and brown sugar until light and fluffy.

2 Use the wooden spoon to beat in the egg and vanilla and mix well.

3 Slowly add the rest of the ingredients one by one. Mix well.

4 Pour the dough into the baking pan and spread evenly. The top should be smooth. Bake for 30 minutes.

5 Remove from the oven and cool before cutting into bars. Makes about 24 bars.

IN THE MICROWAVE ...

Make the dough as directed in steps 1, 2 and 3. Then pour the dough into an ungreased 23 cm (9 in.) round glass baking dish. Microwave on high for 3 to 4 minutes, rotating the dish partway through. When done, a toothpick inserted in the middle should come out clean.

Oatmeal sunflower crispies

These oatmeal cookies have lots of crunch and plenty of flavor. And they're good for you!

YOU WILL NEED

250 mL	soft margarine or butter	1 c.
250 mL	brown sugar	1 c.
750 mL	uncooked large-flake regular oats	3 c.
175 mL	all-purpose flour	¾ c.
5 mL	baking soda	1 tsp.
250 mL	sunflower seeds	1 c.
50 mL	milk	¼ c.

UTENSILS
2 cookie sheets
measuring cups
measuring spoons
wooden spoon
large mixing bowl
spatula

1 Heat the oven to 350°F (180°C) and lightly grease the cookie sheets.

2 Put the margarine or butter and brown sugar into a large bowl and stir until light and fluffy.

3 Mix in the oats, flour, baking soda, sunflower seeds and milk.

4 Use your hands to roll the dough into 2 cm (1 in.) balls.

5 Put the balls about 10 cm (4 in.) apart on the greased cookie sheets and bake for 12 to 15 minutes or until golden brown.

6 Let the crispies cool before lifting them carefully with a spatula. Makes about 36 cookies.

Sunflower power

The sunflower is well named. It really does reach for the sun. Some plants grow as tall as 6 m (20 ft.).

Just the best sugar cookies

The name of these cookies says it all.

YOU WILL NEED

125 mL	soft butter	½ c.
250 mL	sugar	1 c.
2	eggs	
15 mL	lemon juice	1 tbsp.
	grated rind of 1 lemon	
625 mL	all-purpose flour	2 ½ c.
5 mL	baking powder	1 tsp.
1 mL	salt	¼ tsp.
	raisins (optional)	

UTENSILS
measuring cups
measuring spoons
small bowl
large bowl
sifter
knife
2 cookie sheets

1 With a wooden spoon, beat together the butter and sugar in a large bowl until light and creamy.

2 In a small bowl stir together the eggs, lemon juice and rind.

3 In a large bowl sift together the flour, baking powder and salt.

4 Add the egg mixture to the butter mixture. Then add the flour mixture.

5 Cut the dough into 4 pieces. Roll each into a cylinder, wrap in waxed paper and chill for 2 hours.

6 Heat the oven to 375°F (190°C) and lightly grease the cookie sheets.

7 Slice the dough thinly and put the slices on the cookie sheet. Top with raisins if desired.

8 Bake for 10 minutes or until lightly browned. Makes about 48 cookies.

Sweet success

To turn cookies golden brown all over, put them on the middle rack of the oven when you bake them.

Nutty orange balls

These no-bake treats are easy to make — and even easier to eat!

YOU WILL NEED

1	250 g (8 oz.) package vanilla wafers	
1	orange, washed	
125 mL	chopped pecans or other nuts	½ c.
50 mL	honey	¼ c.
1 mL	vanilla	¼ tsp.
50 mL	brown sugar	¼ c.
50 mL	toasted shredded coconut	¼ c.

UTENSILS
plastic bag
rolling pin
medium-sized bowl
grater
knife
measuring cups
measuring spoons
small plate

1 Put the vanilla wafers in a plastic bag and crush them with a rolling pin. Dump the crumbs into a medium-sized bowl.

2 Grate the orange peel and add the grated rind to the crumbs.

3 Slice the orange in half and squeeze the juice from the halves into the crumb mixture. Don't let any seeds slip in.

4 Stir in the nuts, honey and vanilla and mix well.

5 Mix the brown sugar and toasted coconut together on a small plate.

6 Use your hands to shape the cookie mixture into bite-sized balls, then roll them in the sugar and coconut mixture. Makes about 24 cookies.

Orange houses

Orangeries were sixteenth- and seventeenth-century greenhouses — lovely houses or rooms of glass designed to grow orange trees indoors.

Candy cookies

YOU WILL NEED

250 mL	softened unsalted butter	1 c.
250 mL	loosely packed brown sugar	1 c.
125 mL	white sugar	½ c.
2	eggs	
7 mL	vanilla	1 ½ tsp.
625 mL	all-purpose flour	2 ½ c.
5 mL	baking soda	1 tsp.
	pinch of salt	
250 mL	candy-covered chocolate pieces such as Smarties or M & M's	1 c.

UTENSILS
measuring cup
large bowl
beater (hand or electric)
measuring spoons
small bowl
teaspoon
2 cookie sheets

1 Heat the oven to 375°F (190°C).

2 Put the butter in a large bowl and beat it with a beater for about 30 seconds.

3 Pour in the brown and white sugar and beat until fluffy.

4 Add the eggs and vanilla and beat well.

5 Mix the flour, baking soda and salt together in a small bowl, then pour them into the large bowl. Beat until well mixed.

6 Stir in the candies and drop teaspoons of dough about 5 cm (2 in.) apart onto ungreased cookie sheets. Flatten the cookies slightly with your hand. Bake for 8 to 10 minutes or until the cookies are very lightly browned. Makes about 36 cookies.

Fat alberts

They look and taste a bit like peanut brittle. Nobody seems to know why they're called what they are, and nobody seems able to guess what's in them when they taste them. One bite, though, and everyone wants more.

YOU WILL NEED

24–28	graham crackers	
250 mL	unsalted butter	1 c.
250 mL	brown sugar	1 c.
500 mL	sliced almonds	2 c.

UTENSILS

cookie sheet	saucepan
measuring cups	wooden spoon

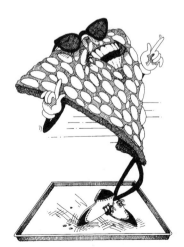

1 Heat the oven to 400°F (200 °C).

2 Cover a cookie sheet with graham crackers. The crackers should be touching one another.

3 Melt the butter over low heat in a saucepan.

4 Stir in the sugar and bring the mixture to a boil. Be careful not to let the mixture boil over.

5 Pour the sugar mixture over all the graham crackers and sprinkle the sliced almonds on top.

6 Bake for 8 minutes or until bubbly. Remove from oven and cool, then slice into squares. Makes about 30 cookies.

IN THE MICROWAVE...

Follow the instructions for step 2, then microwave the butter in a large glass measuring cup on high for 1½ to 2 minutes. Stir in the sugar and microwave for 1 to 2 minutes on high until the mixture boils. Continue with steps 5 and 6.

Octobers

This old recipe dates back to the time when people dried their own apple rings in the fall. Today you can get dried apple rings in health food stores and some supermarkets. They're delicious as they are — or mixed with other ingredients in these special cookies.

YOU WILL NEED

125 mL	soft unsalted butter	½ c.
125 mL	shortening	½ c.
250 mL	brown sugar	1 c.
1	egg, lightly beaten	
5 mL	vanilla	1 tsp.
375 mL	all-purpose flour	1½ c.
2 mL	salt	½ tsp.
2 mL	baking soda	½ tsp.
7 mL	cinnamon	1½ tsp.
2 mL	nutmeg	½ tsp.
375 mL	finely chopped dried apple rings	1½ c.
50 mL	chopped walnuts	¼ c.

UTENSILS

2 cookie sheets	wooden spoon
measuring cups	large bowl
measuring spoons	teaspoon

1 Preheat the oven to 375°F (190°C) and lightly grease the cookie sheets.

2 In a large bowl, cream together the butter, shortening and brown sugar.

3 Stir in the egg and the vanilla and mix well.

4 Add the flour, salt, baking soda, cinnamon, nutmeg, chopped dried apples and chopped nuts. Mix well. Using a teaspoon, drop spoonfuls of dough onto the cookie sheets. Keep each cookie 7 cm (3 in.) apart. Bake 10 to 12 minutes or until cookies are golden. Makes about 48 cookies.

Cocoa shorties

If you crossed Christmas shortbreads with cocoa, you'd get something like these delicious cocoa shorties.

YOU WILL NEED

500 mL	all-purpose flour	2 c.
75 mL	cocoa powder	⅓ c.
2 mL	salt	½ tsp.
175 mL	shortening	¾ c.
125 mL	soft butter	½ c.
325 mL	sifted icing sugar	1⅓ c.
5 mL	vanilla	1 tsp.
75 mL	ground almonds (optional)	⅓ c.

UTENSILS

2 cookie sheets
sifter
measuring cup
measuring spoons
medium-sized bowl
large bowl
wooden spoon
teaspoon

1 Heat the oven to 325°F (160°C) and lightly grease the cookie sheets.

2 Sift the flour, cocoa powder and salt into a medium-sized bowl.

3 In a large bowl, cream the shortening and butter and slowly mix in the icing sugar.

4 Stir in the vanilla and then gradually stir the flour mixture into the butter mixture.

5 When the dough is well mixed, stir in the almonds.

6 Scoop up teaspoons of the dough and form them into tiny patties. Place 1 cm (½ in.) apart on cookie sheets and bake for 12 to 15 minutes. Makes about 36 cookies.

Another hot chocolate, please.

Dried and roasted cocoa beans boiled in water were the first hot chocolate drinks. Even though the taste was very bitter, rumor has it that Montezuma, the Aztec emperor, drank more than 50 cups a day.

Cornflake cookies

These cookies are very crunchy — perfect with fruit for dessert.

YOU WILL NEED

1	egg white	
125 mL	sugar	½ c.
1 mL	vanilla	¼ tsp.
	dash of salt	
125 mL	shredded toasted coconut	½ c.
125 mL	large-flake regular oats	½ c.
250 mL	cornflakes	1 c.

UTENSILS

eggbeater or electric mixer
2 cookie sheets
measuring cups
measuring spoons
2 medium-sized bowls
wooden spoon
teaspoon

1 Heat the oven to 350°F (180°C) and lightly grease the cookie sheets.

2 Beat the egg white with an eggbeater or electric mixer until stiff peaks form, then stir in the sugar, vanilla and salt and beat for a few seconds more.

3 Mix the toasted coconut, oats and cornflakes together in a separate bowl.

4 Mix the egg-white mixture into the cornflake mixture.

5 Scoop up teaspoons of dough and drop them onto the cookie sheets, about 5 cm (2 in.) apart. Bake for about 10 minutes or until lightly browned. Makes about 18 cookies.

Chocolate-chunk cookies

This chunky version of the chocolate-chip cookie is great for school lunches or snacks.

YOU WILL NEED

175 mL	soft butter	¾ c.
250 mL	firmly packed brown sugar	1 c.
1	egg	
2 mL	vanilla	½ tsp.
2 mL	grated orange rind (optional)	½ tsp.
175 mL	all-purpose flour	¾ c.
125 mL	whole wheat flour	½ c.
2 mL	baking soda	½ tsp.
	pinch of salt	
224 g (8 oz.)	sweet baking chocolate or chocolate bars	

UTENSILS
small sharp knife
2 cookie sheets
measuring cups
measuring spoons
large bowl
wooden spoon
teaspoon

1 Heat the oven to 375°F (190°C) and lightly grease the cookie sheets.

2 Put the butter, brown sugar, egg, vanilla and orange rind into a large bowl and beat with a wooden spoon until fluffy.

3 Stir in the white and brown flour, baking soda and salt and mix well.

4 Cut the chocolate bars into Chicklet-sized chunks and stir them into the dough.

5 Drop teaspoons of dough onto the cookie sheets and bake for 10 to 12 minutes or until golden brown. Makes about 24 cookies.

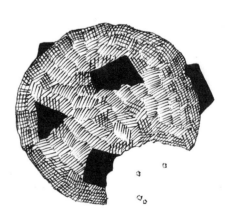

Gingerbread people

This gingerbread recipe is perfect for making cookie people.

YOU WILL NEED

125 mL	soft butter	½ c.
125 mL	brown sugar	½ c.
1	egg	
125 mL	molasses	½ c.
15 mL	vinegar	1 tbsp.
750 mL	all-purpose flour	3 c.
7 mL	powdered ginger	1½ tsp.
5 mL	cinnamon	1 tsp.
2 mL	ground cloves	½ tsp.

UTENSILS

2 cookie sheets	sifter
large bowl	medium-sized bowl
measuring cups	rolling pin
measuring spoons	cookie cutters
wooden spoon	

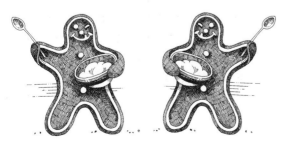

1 In a large bowl, beat the butter and brown sugar with a wooden spoon until smooth.

2 Add the egg, molasses and vinegar and mix well.

3 Sift the flour, ginger, cinnamon and ground cloves together into the medium-sized bowl. Mix these dry ingredients into the egg mixture and blend well.

4 Shape the dough into a ball and wrap it in waxed paper. Put the dough in the refrigerator for at least 2 hours so that it will be easier to roll out.

5 Heat the oven to 375°F (190°C) and lightly grease the cookie sheets.

6 Remove the dough from the fridge and cut it into quarters. Sprinkle the rolling pin and the counter or a pastry board with a little flour so that the dough won't stick. Roll out a piece of the dough until it is about 0.5 cm (⅛ in.) thick.

7 Use your favorite cookie cutters to cut out shapes and place the shapes on the greased cookie sheets.

8 Bake for 10 minutes or until lightly browned. Makes about 36 cookies.

Hello dollies

*These gooey, chewy bars are fast
and easy to make.*

YOU WILL NEED

50 mL	butter	¼ c.
250 mL	fine graham-cracker crumbs	1 c.
250 mL	flaked dried coconut	1 c.
250 mL	chocolate chips	1 c.
1	300 mL (15 oz.) can sweetened condensed milk	

UTENSILS
saucepan
2.5 L (9 in.) square cake pan
measuring cups
fork
can opener

1 Heat the oven to 325°F (160°C).

2 Melt the butter in the saucepan and add the graham-cracker crumbs. Mix well with a fork.

3 Pat the graham crackers into the bottom of the cake pan to make a crust.

4 Sprinkle the crust with coconut, then with chocolate chips.

5 Pour the condensed milk over the chocolate chips.

6 Bake for 30 minutes.

7 Remove from the oven and cool before cutting into squares. Makes 12 to 16 squares.

IN THE MICROWAVE...

Microwave the butter for 45 seconds to 1 minute in a 23 cm (9 in.) round glass baking dish. Add the graham-cracker crumbs and mix well. Continue with steps 3 to 5. Microwave for 7 to 9 minutes on medium, rotating the dish partway through cooking if necessary, until the mixture is set. Let cool before cutting into squares.

Giant peanut-butter cookies

These huge cookies are rolled in the palm of your hands, then flattened with a fork for a crisscross pattern before being baked. They are yummy!

YOU WILL NEED

250 mL	soft butter	1 c.
150 mL	brown sugar	⅔ c.
150 mL	white sugar	⅔ c.
250 mL	chunky peanut butter	1 c.
2	eggs, well beaten	
750 mL	all-purpose flour	3 c.
10 mL	baking soda	2 tsp.
1 mL	salt	¼ tsp.

UTENSILS
2 cookie sheets
wooden spoon
measuring cups
measuring spoons
large bowl
tablespoon
fork

1 Heat the oven to 350°F (180°C) and lightly grease the cookie sheets.

2 In a large bowl, use a wooden spoon to beat the butter until creamy.

3 Slowly add the brown and the white sugars and beat well until blended.

4 Add the peanut butter and beat until soft and fluffy.

5 Stir in the eggs, one at a time, beating well after adding each.

6 Pour the flour into the peanut-butter mixture, then stir in the baking soda and salt. Beat until all the ingredients are mixed. The dough will be crumbly.

7 Scoop up a heaping tablespoon of dough and roll it into a large ball in the palms of your hands. Repeat until all the dough is used up. Place the balls about 2 cm (1 in.) apart on a cookie sheet. Gently flatten each cookie by pressing it with the back of a fork. Make a crisscross pattern on the top.

8 Bake for 10 minutes or until the edges are slightly brown in color. Makes about 24 giant cookies.

CAKES AND PIES

Chocomint brownies

These brownies are gooey inside with a crisp top layer. They're also minty and very sweet.

YOU WILL NEED

250 mL	chocolate-mint chips	1 c.
125 mL	unsalted butter	½ c.
3	eggs at room temperature	
	dash of salt	
5 mL	vanilla	1 tsp.
250 mL	white sugar	1 c.
125 mL	brown sugar	½ c.
175 mL	all-purpose flour	¾ c.
250 mL	broken walnut pieces	1 c.

UTENSILS

2.5 L (9 in.) square cake pan
double boiler

2 medium-sized bowls
wooden spoon
sifter

1 Heat the oven to 350°F (180°C) and prepare the cake pan by lightly greasing it and dusting it with flour.

2 Melt the chocolate chips and the butter over medium heat in the top of the double boiler. (See page 8 for how to use a double boiler.) Mix well, remove from the heat and set aside.

3 In a medium-sized bowl, beat together the eggs, salt and vanilla until light in color.

4 Slowly add the white and brown sugars and continue to beat until the mixture is smooth.

5 Add the melted chocolate mixture and beat until smooth.

6 In another bowl, sift the flour, then gradually stir it into the chocolate mixture.

7 Fold in the nuts and mix well, then spoon the batter into the cake pan. Bake for 50 minutes.

8 Remove from oven and let cool before cutting into squares. Makes about 24 squares.

MICROWAVE TIP

Instead of melting the chocolate chips and butter on the stove, put them in a large glass measuring cup and microwave on medium for 2 to 3 minutes. Stir to help the chocolate melt.

Chocolate buttermilk one-bowl cake

This simple, light cake is so good on its own that no icing is necessary. For a special occasion, you could top it off with whipped cream and sliced fruit.

YOU WILL NEED

3	28 g (1 oz.) squares unsweetened chocolate	
25 mL	water	2 tbsp.
50 mL	soft unsalted butter	¼ c.
175 mL	sugar	¾ c.
250 mL	sifted cake flour	1 c.
75 mL	molasses	⅓ c.
2 mL	baking soda	½ tsp.
2 mL	salt	½ tsp.
2 mL	baking powder	½ tsp.
125 mL	water	½ c.
125 mL	buttermilk	½ c.
1	egg	
5 mL	vanilla	1 tsp.

UTENSILS

1.5 L (9 in.) springform pan
small saucepan
large bowl

electric mixer
spatula or wooden spoon
knife

1 Heat the oven to 350°F (180°C) and prepare the springform pan by lightly greasing it and dusting it with flour.

2 Put the chocolate and water in the saucepan and stir over low heat until melted. Set aside.

3 In the large bowl, use the wooden spoon to mix the butter and sugar together until creamy.

4 Add the melted chocolate, then the remaining ingredients. Using an electric mixer, beat on medium speed until smooth and fluffy — about 3 to 5 minutes.

5 Pour the batter into the springform pan and smooth the top with a spatula or wooden spoon.

6 Bake for 45 minutes or until a knife inserted in the center comes out clean.

7 Remove the cake from the oven and set aside to cool. When the cake is cool, release the sides of the springform pan and put the cake on a plate. Serves six.

MICROWAVE TIP

Instead of melting the chocolate and water on the stove, put them in a large glass measuring cup and microwave on medium for 2 to 3 minutes. Stir to help the chocolate melt.

Tomato soup cake

Your friends won't believe the secret ingredient in this cake. But one taste and they'll want more. Perhaps it tastes so good because tomatoes are actually fruits.

YOU WILL NEED

50 mL	soft butter	¼ c.
250 mL	sugar	1 c.
1	egg	
1	284 mL (10 oz) can tomato soup	
125 mL	all-purpose flour	½ c.
1 mL	salt	¼ tsp.
10 mL	baking soda	2 tsp.
2 mL	cinnamon	½ tsp.
2 mL	nutmeg	½ tsp.
1 mL	allspice	¼ tsp.
1 mL	ground cloves	¼ tsp.
125 mL	chopped walnuts (optional)	½ c.
125 mL	seedless raisins	½ c.
	cream cheese frosting (page 60)	

UTENSILS

2.0 L (8 in.) square cake pan
measuring cups
measuring spoons

wooden spoon
2 medium-sized mixing bowls
sifter

1 Heat the oven to 350°F (180°C) and prepare the cake pan by lightly greasing it and dusting it with flour.

2 In a mixing bowl, stir together the butter, sugar and egg and mix well.

3 Add the tomato soup straight from the can.

4 In another bowl, sift together the flour, salt, baking soda, cinnamon, nutmeg, allspice and ground cloves.

5 Add the flour mixture to the tomato-soup mixture and mix well.

6 Stir in the walnuts and raisins and then spread the batter evenly in the cake pan. Bake for about 50 minutes or until a knife inserted in the center comes out clean.

7 Remove from oven and allow to cool completely before spreading on cream cheese frosting. Serves eight.

Pistachio carrot cake

Pistachios add color and crunch to this moist cake. (You can substitute walnuts or leave the nuts out if you wish.)

YOU WILL NEED

250 mL	all-purpose flour	1 c.
5 mL	baking powder	1 tsp.
1 mL	salt	¼ tsp.
2	eggs	
1 mL	crushed cardamom (optional)	¼ tsp.
250 mL	brown sugar	1 c.
50 mL	melted butter	¼ c.
375 mL	grated carrots	1½ c.
25 mL	shelled, chopped pistachios	2 tbsp.
50 mL	raisins (optional)	¼ c.
	cream cheese frosting (page 60)	

UTENSILS

2.0 L (8 in.) square cake pan	medium-sized bowl
measuring cups	large bowl
measuring spoons	grater
sifter	wooden spoon
	knife or toothpick

1 Heat the oven to 350°F (180°C) and prepare the cake pan by lightly greasing it and dusting it with flour.

2 Sift the flour, baking powder and salt into a medium-sized bowl.

3 In a large bowl, beat the eggs with a wooden spoon, then add the cardamom, brown sugar and butter. Mix well.

4 Slowly stir the dry ingredients into the egg mixture, then mix in the rest of the ingredients.

5 Pour the batter into the cake pan and bake for 55 minutes or until a knife inserted in the center comes out clean.

6 Remove from the oven and allow to cool completely before spreading on the cream cheese frosting. Serves eight to ten.

IN THE MICROWAVE...

Follow the instructions for steps 2 to 4, then pour the batter into an ungreased 23 cm (9 in.) round glass baking dish. Microwave for 4 minutes on medium, then 3 to 4 minutes on high or until a toothpick inserted in the center comes out clean. Continue with step 6.

Cinnamon pear cake

Wonderful with cocoa or tea, as breakfast or as a snack, this coffee cake takes only a few minutes to mix up.

YOU WILL NEED

CAKE

2	eggs	
250 mL	sugar	1 c.
125 mL	vegetable oil	½ c.
2 mL	vanilla	½ tsp.
375 mL	all-purpose flour	1 ½ c.
15 mL	baking powder	1 tbsp.
1 mL	salt	¼ tsp.
125 mL	orange juice	½ c.

TOPPING

125 mL	brown sugar	½ c.
10 mL	cinnamon	2 tsp.
15 mL	all-purpose flour	1 tbsp.
50 mL	vegetable oil	¼ c.
1	ripe pear, peeled, cored and thinly sliced	

UTENSILS

2.0 L (8 in.) square cake pan
measuring cups
measuring spoons

large bowl
small bowl
wooden spoon

1 Heat the oven to 350°F (180°C) and prepare the cake pan by lightly greasing it and dusting it with flour.

2 To make the cake, mix the eggs, sugar, oil and vanilla together in a large bowl.

3 Stir in the flour, baking powder, salt and orange juice.

4 In a small bowl, make the topping by mixing together the brown sugar, cinnamon, flour and vegetable oil. The topping should be crumbly.

5 Pour the cake batter into the cake pan and sprinkle the topping over it. Arrange the sliced pears on top. Bake for 30 minutes. Serves six.

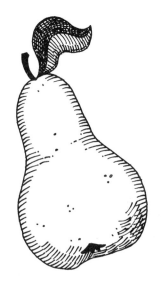

Nanaimo bars

YOU WILL NEED

BOTTOM LAYER

125 mL	unsalted butter	½ c.
1	egg	
2 mL	vanilla	½ tsp.
25 mL	cocoa	2 tbsp.
250 mL	crushed unsalted peanuts	1 c.
500 mL	graham-cracker crumbs	2 c.

MIDDLE LAYER

50 mL	custard powder	3 tbsp.
500 mL	icing sugar	2 c.
50 mL	soft unsalted butter	¼ c.
50 mL	milk	¼ c.

TOP LAYER

1	175 g (8 oz.) package semisweet chocolate chips	
25 mL	soft unsalted butter	2 tbsp.

UTENSILS

double boiler

measuring spoons

measuring cups

plastic bag

rolling pin or blender

medium-sized bowl

wooden spoon

2.5 L (9 in.) square cake pan

knife

BOTTOM LAYER

1 Mix the butter, egg, vanilla and cocoa together and heat in the top of a double boiler. Stir until the mixture is slightly thickened, then set it aside.

2 Crush the peanuts with a rolling pin or in a blender.

3 Stir the crushed peanuts and graham-cracker crumbs into the cocoa mixture.

4 When it is cool, press the batter into the bottom of the cake pan and chill in the fridge for 10 minutes.

MIDDLE LAYER

1 Mix all the ingredients together in a bowl.

2 Spread this mixture over the bottom layer and chill for another 10 minutes.

TOP LAYER

1 Melt the chocolate and butter in the top of a double boiler.

2 Spread this over the middle layer and chill for 1 to 2 hours. Cut into 24 squares.

IN THE MICROWAVE...

BOTTOM LAYER: Put the butter, egg, vanilla and cocoa into a large microwavable bowl and microwave for 2 to 4 minutes at medium heat until slightly thickened. Stir partway through. Continue with steps 3, 4 and 5.

MIDDLE LAYER: Same as above.

TOP LAYER: Microwave the chocolate chips and butter in a microwavable measuring cup on medium for 3 to 4 minutes. Stir to help melting. Continue with step 2.

Peanut-butter candy cheesecake

This cheesecake, studded with Reese's Pieces, is terrific for special birthday parties.

YOU WILL NEED

25 mL	unsalted butter	2 tbsp.
250 mL	graham-cracker crumbs	1 c.
50 mL	sugar	3 tbsp.
600 g	cream cheese	1¼ lb.
50 mL	cold unsalted butter, cut into 8 pieces	3 tbsp.
250 mL	sugar	1 c.
3	large eggs	
2 mL	vanilla	½ tsp.
1	small package Reese's Pieces	

UTENSILS

measuring cups
measuring spoons
wooden spoon
small saucepan
hand mixer or
  electric mixer

large mixing bowl
1.3 L (8 in.)
  springform pan
  or deep pie plate

1 Put the 25 mL (2 tbsp.) butter in a saucepan and melt it over low heat on the stove.

2 Remove the melted butter from the heat and add the cracker crumbs and the 50 mL (3 tbsp.) sugar. Mix well with a wooden spoon, then press the crumb mixture into the bottom of a springform pan or deep pie plate to make a crust.

3 Heat the oven to 350°F (180°C).

4 In a large mixing bowl, use a hand mixer or electric mixer to beat the cream cheese, butter and sugar together until light and smooth.

5 Add the eggs and vanilla and continue beating until thoroughly mixed.

6 Pour the cheesecake mixture over the graham-cracker crust and sprinkle on the Reese's Pieces. Use a wooden spoon to gently fold the candy into the batter.

7 Bake for 25 to 30 minutes or until the edges of the cake have puffed up slightly. Remove the cheesecake from oven and allow to cool to room temperature. Refrigerate until ready to serve. Makes eight to ten large servings.

Maple nut pie

This is an easy no-bake version of Quebec's famous maple sugar pie. Since this dessert is very, very sweet, small servings are recommended.

YOU WILL NEED

CRUST
325 mL	graham-cracker crumbs	1½ c.
75 mL	melted butter	⅓ c.
25 mL	crushed walnuts	2 tbsp.

FILLING
1	300 mL (12 oz.) can sweetened condensed milk	
125 mL	maple syrup	½ c.
125 mL	chopped walnuts	½ c.
2 mL	vanilla	½ tsp.

TOPPING (OPTIONAL)
125 mL	whipping cream	½ c.
1	small chocolate bar	

UTENSILS

measuring cups
measuring spoons
2 wooden spoons
medium-sized pot
eggbeater or electric mixer

1.0 L (9 in.) pie plate
medium-sized bowl
grater

CRUST

1 Mix together the graham-cracker crumbs, melted butter and nuts in a mixing bowl.

2 Use your hands to press the mixture into the bottom and sides of a pie plate. Make sure that the thickness is the same all around. Chill in refrigerator for 30 minutes.

FILLING

1 Put the milk and maple syrup in the pot and heat to a gentle boil over medium heat. Cook, stirring, until thick — about 5 minutes.

2 Mix in the walnuts and the vanilla and set the pot aside to cool for 10 minutes.

3 Pour the maple filling over the chilled piecrust. When the filling is cool, refrigerate the pie for at least 1 hour.

TOPPING

1 Whip the cream with an eggbeater or electric mixer. Spread it over the pie just before serving.

2 Grate the chocolate bar into shavings and sprinkle these over the whipped cream. Serves eight to ten.

Chocolate sundae pie

When kids at Deer Park Junior High in Toronto were asked to name their favorite desserts, chocolate sundaes were mentioned again and again. This delicious no-bake pie is a chocolate sundae plus! (You can also make it with any other flavor of ice cream.)

YOU WILL NEED

1	250 g (8 oz.) package chocolate wafers	
50 mL	margarine or butter	¼ c.
1 L	of your favorite ice cream	4 c.
125 mL	chopped walnuts	½ c.
6 or 7	maraschino cherries	
	chocolate sauce (recipe page 61 or use bottled sauce)	

UTENSILS

plastic bag	large spoon
rolling pin	spatula
bowl	1.0 L (9 in.)
saucepan	pie plate

1 Put the chocolate wafers in a plastic bag and crush them with a rolling pin. Pour them into a bowl.

2 In a small saucepan, melt the margarine or butter over low heat.

3 Pour the margarine or butter over the crushed wafers. Mix well, then use your hands to press the crushed-wafer mixture into a crust in the bottom of a pie plate.

4 Put the pie plate with the crust in the freezer and chill for 15 minutes. When the crust goes into the freezer, take out the ice cream. This will let the ice cream soften slightly before you need to use it.

5 When the piecrust has chilled for 15 minutes, remove it from the freezer and spoon or scoop the slightly softened ice cream over it. Use a spatula or the back of a spoon run under hot water to smooth the ice cream over the pie.

6 Sprinkle the top with chopped walnuts and decorate with cherries, then freeze until firm. Serve with chocolate sauce. Serves eight to ten.

Fruity pizza pie

YOU WILL NEED

BOTTOM LAYER

375 mL	all-purpose flour	1½ c.
50 mL	sugar	¼ c.
	pinch of salt	
175 mL	soft butter	¾ c.
7 mL	white vinegar	1½ tsp.

MIDDLE LAYER

1	250 g (8 oz.) package cream cheese at room temperature	
15 mL	sugar	1 tbsp.
2 mL	vanilla	½ tsp.
50 mL	milk	3 tbsp.

TOP LAYER

2	apples, cored and sliced thinly	
5 mL	lemon juice	1 tsp.
2	bananas, peeled and sliced thinly	
2	oranges, peeled and sliced thinly	
15 to 20	green seedless grapes, cut in half	
1	26 g (1 oz.) square semisweet baking chocolate	

UTENSILS

measuring cups
measuring spoons
wooden spoon
2 large bowls
spatula

wire whisk or
  electric mixer
pizza pan
  or cookie sheet
grater

BOTTOM LAYER

1 In a mixing bowl, stir together the flour, sugar and salt.

2 Bit by bit, mix in the butter and vinegar. Use a spoon or your hands to mix the dough until it looks like cookie dough.

3 Pat the dough onto the bottom of a pizza pan. Or make a large circle of dough on a cookie sheet. Make sure the crust is the same thickness all over.

4 Chill the crust in the fridge for 30 minutes.

5 Heat the oven to 350°F (180°C) and bake the crust for about 15 minutes, until golden brown. Set aside to cool to room temperature.

MIDDLE LAYER

1 Put the cream cheese, sugar, vanilla and milk into a bowl and use a wire whisk or electric mixer to mix until very smooth.

2 Spread the cream cheese mixture over the cooled crust with a spatula and refrigerate for 30 minutes.

TOP LAYER

1 Sprinkle the sliced apples with lemon juice to prevent them from turning brown.

2 Arrange the apples, bananas, oranges and grapes in any pattern you wish on top of the cream cheese.

3 Grate the chocolate and sprinkle it over the top. Serves 10 to 12.

Lemon angel pie

YOU WILL NEED

BOTTOM LAYER

4	egg whites	
1 mL	cream of tartar	¼ tsp.
250 mL	sugar	1 c.

TOP LAYER

4	egg yolks	
125 mL	sugar	½ c.
	juice and rind of 1 lemon	
250 mL	whipping cream	1 c.
5 mL	vanilla	1 tsp.
15 mL	toasted shredded coconut (optional)	1 tbsp.

UTENSILS

3 medium-sized mixing bowls	measuring cups
	measuring spoons
eggbeater or electric mixer	1.0 L (9 in.) pie plate
wooden spoon	

BOTTOM LAYER

1 Heat the oven to 300°F (150°C) and lightly grease a pie plate with a bit of vegetable oil.

2 Beat the egg whites with an eggbeater or electric mixer until foamy.

3 Add the cream of tartar and continue to beat the eggs until soft, moist peaks form.

4 Gradually add the sugar, about 25 mL (2 tbsp.) at a time, and continue to beat until the egg whites form stiff, glossy peaks.

5 Use a wooden spoon to gently pile the eggs into the pie plate. Bake for 1 hour.

TOP LAYER

1 Use an eggbeater or electric mixer to beat the yolks until they are thick.

2 Add the sugar, lemon juice and lemon rind and mix well.

3 Pour the mixture into the top of a double boiler. (See page 8 for how to use a double boiler.) Cook over hot water on low heat until the mixture thickens. Stir constantly. When thickened, remove the mixture from the heat and set aside to cool.

4 In another bowl, use an eggbeater or electric mixer to beat the cream and vanilla until the cream has whipped.

5 Carefully spread the whipped cream over the cooled bottom layer.

6 Pour the lemon mixture over the top. Decorate, if you wish, with toasted coconut. Chill in refrigerator at least 4 hours or overnight. Serves eight.

MUFFINS AND BREADS

Chocolate-chip banana-split muffins

This recipe calls for chocolate chips, but you can substitute butterscotch, even orange-flavored chocolate chips, if you wish.

YOU WILL NEED

250 mL	all-purpose flour	1 c.
250 mL	whole-wheat flour	1 c.
15 mL	baking powder	1 tbsp.
2 mL	salt	½ tsp.
125 mL	chocolate chips	½ c.
1	mashed banana	
25 mL	chopped maraschino cherries	2 tbsp.
1	egg, slightly beaten	
75 mL	sunflower seed or corn oil	⅓ c.
250 mL	milk	1 c.
50 mL	molasses	¼ c.

UTENSILS
muffin pans for 12 muffins
paper muffin-pan liners (optional)
2 medium-sized mixing bowls
measuring cups
measuring spoons
wooden spoon
knife

1 Heat the oven to 400°F (200°C). Prepare the muffin pans by either greasing the muffin cups or lining them with paper muffin-pan liners.

2 In a medium-sized bowl, mix together the all-purpose flour, whole-wheat flour, baking powder and salt.

3 In another medium-sized bowl, mix together the chocolate chips, banana, cherries, egg, oil, milk and molasses.

4 Add the flour mixture to the other mixture, mixing only enough to moisten. (Do not overmix.) Fill the prepared muffin cups about two-thirds full and bake for 15 to 20 minutes or until a knife inserted in the center of a muffin comes out clean. Makes 12–18 muffins.

Corn muffins

Visit the southern United States and you'll find that cornbread or corn muffins are part of every dinner. Because they're not very sweet, you might want to spoon on some jam or honey before you eat them. If you're not going to eat these right away, store them in a plastic bag or wrap them in plastic wrap so they don't dry out.

YOU WILL NEED

300 mL	milk	1¼ c.
25 mL	honey	2 tbsp.
25 mL	raisins	2 tbsp.
5 mL	grated lemon rind	1 tsp.
50 mL	butter	¼ c.
375 mL	all-purpose flour	1½ c.
175 mL	yellow cornmeal	¾ c.
15 mL	baking powder	1 tbsp.
2 mL	salt	½ tsp.

UTENSILS

measuring cups
measuring spoons
wooden spoon
saucepan
paper muffin-pan
  liners (optional)

muffin pans
  for 12 muffins
2 medium-sized
  bowls
knife

1 Heat the oven to 425°F (220°C). Prepare the muffin pans by either greasing the muffin cups or lining them with paper muffin-pan liners.

2 Put the milk, honey, raisins and lemon rind into a medium-sized bowl and mix well.

3 Put the butter in a saucepan and melt it over low heat. When it is melted, pour it into the milk and raisin mixture and mix well.

4 Put the flour, cornmeal, baking powder and salt into another bowl and mix.

5 Gently spoon the wet mixture into the dry ingredients, mixing only enough to moisten. (Do not overmix.) Fill the prepared muffin cups about two-thirds full and bake for 20 minutes or until a knife inserted in the center of a muffin comes out clean. Makes 12 muffins.

Apple cheddar muffins

Try this with your favorite fall apples. We especially like Granny Smiths for a tart, refreshing flavor, or McIntoshes for a sweeter taste.

YOU WILL NEED

325 mL	sugar	1⅓ c.
250 mL	unsalted butter	1 c.
4	eggs	
6	large apples, peeled, cored and diced	
500 mL	grated cheddar cheese	2 c.
1 L	all-purpose flour	4 c.
10 mL	baking powder	2 tsp.
5 mL	baking soda	1 tsp.
5 mL	cinnamon	1 tsp.
2 mL	allspice	½ tsp.

UTENSILS

paper muffin-pan liners (optional)
muffin pans for 18 muffins
measuring cups
measuring spoons

large mixing bowl
small mixing bowl
wooden spoon
sifter
knife

1 Heat the oven to 350°F (180°C). Prepare the muffins pans by either greasing the muffin cups or lining them with paper muffin-pan liners.

2 In a large bowl, mix the sugar and butter together until light and fluffy.

3 Stir in the eggs, one at a time, then mix in the diced apples and grated cheese.

4 In a smaller bowl, sift together the flour, baking powder, baking soda, cinnamon and allspice.

5 Add the dry ingredients to the wet, mixing only enough to moisten. (Do not overmix.) Fill the prepared muffin pans about two-thirds full and bake for 25 minutes or until a knife inserted in the center of a muffin comes out clean. Makes 18 muffins.

Yak yogurt?

Did you know that yogurt is one of the world's oldest foods? Centuries ago the most popular yogurts were not made from cow's milk but from the milk of goats, buffalo, even yaks!

Poppy-seed banana bread

Spread this bread with jam for breakfast or eat it with yogurt and fruit any time.

YOU WILL NEED

2	medium bananas	
125 mL	butter or margarine	½ c.
5 mL	vanilla	1 tsp.
175 mL	sugar	¾ c.
2	eggs	
5 mL	lemon juice	1 tsp.
500 mL	sifted all-purpose flour	2 c.
5 mL	salt	1 tsp.
5 mL	baking soda	1 tsp.
125 mL	poppy seeds	½ c.

UTENSILS
measuring cups
measuring spoons
small bowl
wooden spoon
fork or potato masher
2 medium-sized bowls
2.0 L (9 x 5 in.) loaf pan
knife

1 Heat the oven to 350°F (180°C). Lightly grease the loaf pan and dust it with flour.

2 Mash the bananas in a small bowl with a fork or potato masher.

3 In a medium-sized bowl, mix together the butter or margarine, vanilla and sugar until light and fluffy.

4 Gradually beat in the eggs, mashed bananas and lemon juice one after the other.

5 In another bowl, sift together the flour, salt and baking soda. Add the poppy seeds.

6 Mix the dry ingredients with the wet ones, then spoon the batter into the loaf pan. Bake for 50 minutes or until a knife inserted in the center comes out clean. Makes one loaf.

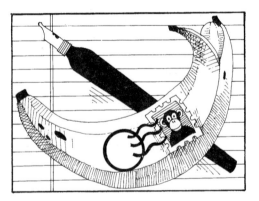

Write-on bananas

Bananas are not only delicious to eat; their leaves contain a fiber that can be made into paper.

Orange bread

This is called a quick bread because there's no yeast in it so it's quick to make. For best results, begin and end with the flour mixture when you're mixing ingredients in step 5.

YOU WILL NEED

75 mL	unsalted butter	⅓ c.
250 mL	sugar	1 c.
	rind of 1 orange, grated	
2	eggs	
375 mL	all-purpose flour	1½ c.
2 mL	salt	½ tsp.
10 mL	baking powder	2 tsp.
50 mL	orange juice	¼ c.
	orange glaze (page 60)	

UTENSILS
measuring cups
measuring spoons
large mixing bowl
sifter
medium-sized mixing bowl
2.0 L (9 x 5 in.) loaf pan
wire whisk or wooden spoon
knife

1 Heat the oven to 350°F (180°C) and lightly grease a loaf pan.

2 In a large bowl, mix together the butter and the sugar until creamy.

3 Stir in the orange rind and beat in the eggs one by one with a wire whisk or wooden spoon.

4 Sift together the flour, salt and baking powder into another bowl.

5 Mix the dry ingredients and the orange juice into the egg mixture bit by bit. For best results, begin and end with the dry ingredients.

6 Pour the batter into a loaf pan and bake for 50 minutes or until a knife inserted in the center comes out clean.

7 Pour the orange glaze over the loaf while it is still hot or warm. Allow it to cool before removing from the pan and slicing. Makes one loaf.

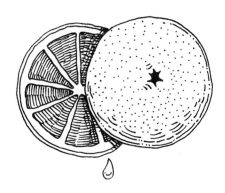

Honey cake

Honey cake with a spoonful of yogurt on top makes a yummy breakfast. With a scoop of ice cream or sliced fresh fruits, it's a delicious dessert!

YOU WILL NEED

250 mL	seedless raisins	1 c.
250 mL	water	1 c.
125 mL	vegetable oil	½ c.
1	egg	
175 mL	liquid honey	¾ c.
425 mL	all-purpose flour	1¾ c.
1 mL	salt	¼ tsp.
5 mL	baking soda	1 tsp.
5 mL	cinnamon	1 tsp.
5 mL	nutmeg	1 tsp.
2 mL	allspice	½ tsp.
2 mL	ground cloves	½ tsp.

UTENSILS
3.0 L (9 x 12 in.) loaf pan
large saucepan
measuring cups
measuring spoons
wooden spoon
medium-sized mixing bowl

1 Heat the oven to 375°F (190°C) and lightly grease the loaf pan.

2 Put the raisins, water and oil in a large saucepan over high heat and bring to a boil. Remove from heat and let stand for 10 minutes.

3 Add the egg and honey to the raisin mixture and mix well.

4 In a bowl, stir together the rest of the ingredients.

5 Add the flour mixture to the raisin mixture and stir until well mixed.

6 Pour the batter into the greased loaf pan and bake for 20 to 25 minutes or until a knife inserted in the center comes out clean. Remove from the oven and cool completely in the pan. Makes one large cake.

MICROWAVE TIP

Instead of boiling the raisins, water and oil in a saucepan, put them in a large measuring cup and microwave on high for 3 to 5 minutes.

SNACKS AND SHAKES

Nutty popcorn

Tie a bag full of this caramel corn with a ribbon for a great party favor.

YOU WILL NEED

125 mL	butter	½ c.
125 mL	liquid honey	½ c.
5 mL	salt	1 tsp.
3 L	popcorn, popped	12 c.
175 mL	unsalted peanuts	¾ c.

UTENSILS
measuring cups
measuring spoons
small saucepan
large bowl
wooden spoon
cookie sheet

1 Heat the oven to 350°F (180°C) and lightly grease the cookie sheet.

2 Melt the butter in a small saucepan over low heat, then stir in the honey and salt.

3 In a large bowl, mix together the popcorn and nuts. Pour on the melted honey-butter and mix well.

4 Spread the popcorn over a cookie sheet in a thin layer, then bake until crisp — about 20 or 25 minutes. Stir occasionally as the popcorn bakes.

5 When cool, break the popcorn into chunks. Store in a covered container in a cool, dry place. Makes about 3 L (12 c.) of popcorn.

MICROWAVE TIP

Instead of melting the butter in a saucepan on the stove, put it in a glass measuring cup and microwave it for 45 seconds to 1 minute on high.

Wearable popcorn

It was the ancient Incas who were first to discover popcorn; they used it for decoration. But it was Native North Americans who discovered it tasted great and introduced the Pilgrims to it.

Crispy nuts

If you don't like one of the nuts suggested in this recipe, you could use less of them and more of ones you especially like. This snack makes a good gift too when put in a clean jam jar and topped with a bow.

1 Heat the oven to 275°F (140°C) and lightly grease the cookie sheet.

2 Put all the nuts in a large bowl and add the sugar, salt, cinnamon and ginger. Toss well.

3 In a small bowl, beat the egg white and water with a fork until foamy. Pour the egg mixture over the nuts and mix well. Make sure to coat all the nuts with egg so that they crisp evenly as they bake.

4 Spread the nuts over the cookie sheet and bake for 35 minutes.

5 When cool, break the nuts into chunks. Store, tightly covered, in an airtight container. Makes about 750 mL (3 c.) of nuts.

YOU WILL NEED

250 mL	whole almonds with their skins	1 c.
250 mL	broken walnut pieces	1 c.
125 mL	unsalted peanuts	½ c.
125 mL	pecan halves	½ c.
125 mL	sugar	½ c.
5 mL	salt	1 tsp.
15 mL	ground cinnamon	1 tbsp.
1 mL	ground ginger	¼ tsp.
1	egg white	
15 mL	water	1 tbsp.

UTENSILS

measuring cups   measuring spoons
large bowl   small bowl
fork   wooden spoon
cookie sheet

Crunchy granola

Who says granola is only for breakfast? A handful any time of day makes a tasty, nourishing snack.

YOU WILL NEED

750 mL	uncooked large-flake regular oats	3 c.
250 mL	wheat germ (optional)	1 c.
250 mL	raisins	1 c.
250 mL	nuts (almonds, walnuts or pecans)	1 c.
125 mL	shredded coconut (optional)	½ c.
75 mL	brown sugar	⅓ c.
125 mL	honey	½ c.
5 mL	vanilla	1 tsp.
1 mL	cinnamon	¼ tsp.
75 mL	vegetable oil	⅓ c.

UTENSILS
measuring cups
measuring spoons
large bowl
wooden spoon
cookie sheet

1 Heat the oven to 300°F (150°C).

2 Mix all the ingredients in a large bowl and spread evenly over a cookie sheet.

3 Bake for 1 hour or until toasted, stirring occasionally.

4 When cool, stir until crumbly. Store in a tightly covered container in the refrigerator. Makes about 1.5 L (6 c.) of granola.

Busy as a …

Bees must collect the nectar of about two million flowers to produce 450 g (1 lb.) of honey. During a worker bee's lifespan, which is about four weeks, it only collects one teaspoonful of nectar.

Peanut butter and banana milk shake

YOU WILL NEED

2	ice cubes	
1	banana, sliced	
50 mL	peanut butter	¼ c.
250 mL	cold milk	1 c.
1	scoop vanilla ice cream	
1 mL	vanilla	¼ tsp.

UTENSILS
measuring cups
measuring spoons
blender
2 glasses

1 Blend the ice cubes, banana, peanut butter, cold milk, ice cream and vanilla in a blender for about half a minute.

2 Pour into glasses. Makes two milk shakes.

Iced tea punch

This tastes like fruity iced tea and is easy to make. You can use any fruit juice and sliced fruits you like.

YOU WILL NEED

750 mL	water	3 c.
2	tea bags	
750 mL	apple or orange juice	3 c.
1	lime, thinly sliced	
1	orange, thinly sliced	
	a handful of berries	

UTENSILS
teapot
pitcher
wooden spoon

1 Boil the water and pour it into a teapot with the tea bags. Steep for 5 minutes, then remove the tea bags.

2 Pour the tea into a large pitcher and add the rest of the ingredients. Stir, then refrigerate for 4 to 24 hours. Makes enough for six.

Melon milk shake

Try this melon smoothie for a dessert or summer breakfast.

YOU WILL NEED

½	cantaloupe or honeydew melon, peeled, seeded and chopped into chunks	
50 mL	frozen orange juice concentrate	¼ c.
500 mL	cold milk	2 c.
50 mL	cold water	¼ c.
25 mL	honey	2 tbsp.
1	scoop vanilla ice cream	

UTENSILS

measuring cups	measuring spoons
knife	blender
ice-cream scoop or large spoon	4 glasses

1 Put all of the ingredients in a blender and blend until smooth — about half a minute.

2 Pour into glasses. Makes four milk shakes.

Coffee milk shake

This one-person milk shake is a great way to use up leftover coffee.

YOU WILL NEED

250 mL	cold coffee	1 c.
1	banana, peeled and sliced	
125 mL	vanilla ice cream	½ c.

UTENSILS
blender
1 glass

1 Put the ingredients into a blender and blend until smooth. Pour into a glass.

Tropical fruit shake

This milk shake doesn't contain any ice cream. But the ice cubes in it will cool you down on even the hottest days.

YOU WILL NEED

250 mL	canned apricot nectar	1 c.
15 mL	lime juice	1 tbsp.
2	kiwi fruit, peeled and sliced	
1	banana, peeled and sliced	
5 mL	honey	1 tsp.
4	ice cubes	
4	strawberries (optional)	

UTENSILS

measuring cups	measuring spoons
blender	4 glasses
small, sharp knife	

1 Put all of the ingredients in a blender and blend until smooth, for about half a minute.

2 Pour into glasses. Top each with a strawberry if you like. Makes four milk shakes.

Real lemonade with mint

Sure, you can buy lemonade in a can or a bottle. But this homemade lemonade is a treat worth trying.

YOU WILL NEED

125 mL	freshly squeezed lemon juice	½ c.
125 mL	sugar	½ c.
875 mL	cold water	3½ c.
	ice cubes	
	a handful of fresh mint (optional)	

UTENSILS
large pitcher
wooden spoon

1 Stir all the ingredients together in a pitcher. Makes enough for four.

Frozen apricot yogurt

As a change from ice cream, frozen yogurt can't be beat. The secret to this one's smoothness is simple — baby food!

YOU WILL NEED

213 mL (7½ oz.) jar apricot junior baby food		
250 mL	orange juice	1 c.
25 mL	honey	2 tbsp.
5 mL	grated orange rind	1 tsp.
500 mL	unflavored yogurt	2 c.

UTENSILS

measuring cups
measuring spoons
mixing bowl
wooden spoon

metal cake pan or 2 metal ice-cube trays
potato masher

1 Combine all the ingredients in a mixing bowl and mix with a wooden spoon until smooth.

2 Spoon into the cake pan or ice-cube trays and freeze for about 2 hours.

3 Let stand at room temperature for 15 minutes, then mash with a potato masher and spoon into bowls. Serves six.

Fruity shootie

This refreshing drink is actually homemade soda pop.

YOU WILL NEED

½	cantaloupe, seeds and rind removed	
8	strawberries, washed, hulled and sliced	
1	banana, peeled and sliced sprinkle of lemon juice	
5 mL	honey	1 tsp.
250 mL	sparkling mineral water	1 c.
250 mL	ice cubes	1 c.

UTENSILS
knife
blender
2 glasses

1 Cut the cantaloupe into bite-sized chunks.

2 Put all the ingredients into the blender and blend until smooth. Pour into two glasses.

Banana split

Ice cream (any flavors) and bananas are the basic ingredients for a banana split. From then on you're on your own. Let your imagination run wild and add any (or all!) of the ingredients listed.

YOU WILL NEED

canned crushed pineapple
strawberry jam
chocolate sauce
whipped cream
chopped nuts
grated coconut
maraschino cherries
kiwi slices
mango slices
strawberries

UTENSILS
ice-cream scoop
knife
large dessert dish or soup bowl
2 spoons!

1 Put scoops of ice cream in the bottom of a dish (three scoops will usually serve two people).

2 Add on whatever you want. You can even make a banana-split boat like this:

or an animal:

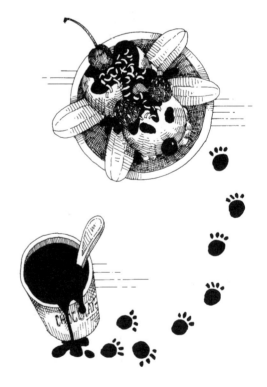

Black-and-white fudge

Marshmallows and chocolate make this a gooey, yummy treat. A little goes a long way.

YOU WILL NEED

500 mL	semisweet chocolate chips	2 c.
425 mL	sweetened condensed milk	1¾ c.
15 mL	cocoa powder	1 tbsp.
5 mL	vanilla	1 tsp.
50 mL	chopped walnuts	¼ c.
4 to 6	marshmallows, chopped into bits	
50 mL	toasted coconut (optional)	¼ c.

UTENSILS
2.5 L (9 in.) square cake pan
measuring spoon
measuring cup
medium-sized saucepan
wooden spoon

1 Lightly grease the cake pan.

2 Melt the chocolate chips over very low heat in a saucepan. Stir constantly to avoid burning.

3 Gradually stir in the condensed milk, cocoa powder, vanilla, walnuts and chopped marshmallows. Mix well.

4 Pour the fudge into a cake pan and smooth the top with a spoon. Sprinkle on the toasted coconut.

5 Refrigerate for about three hours or until firm, then cut into squares. Makes about 24 squares.

MICROWAVE TIP

Instead of melting the chocolate chips on the stove, put them in a large glass measuring cup and microwave on medium for 4 to 6 minutes. Stir to help the chocolate melt.

Chocolate fondue

This dessert is fun to make with friends. While one person melts the chocolate and mixes up the fondue, the others can prepare the fruits and cookies. Though the fondue can be made ahead of time and reheated, most people want to eat it right away.

YOU WILL NEED

125 mL	unsalted butter	½ c.
150 mL	sugar	⅔ c.
125 mL	cocoa powder	½ c.
150 mL	evaporated milk	⅔ c.
5 mL	grated orange peel	1 tsp.
2	bananas, sliced	
1	orange, sectioned	
2	apples, sliced	
	digestive cookies, graham crackers or animal crackers	

UTENSILS

measuring cups	measuring spoons
small saucepan	wooden spoon
large dish	fondue forks

1 Melt the butter in a saucepan over low heat.

2 Stir in the sugar, cocoa powder and evaporated milk. Cook over low heat, stirring constantly, until the sugar is dissolved and the fondue is smooth and chocolaty.

3 Mix in the grated orange peel.

4 Arrange the fruits and cookies on a large plate. Spear fruit on fondue forks and dip into sauce and eat. When the fruit is gone and the fondue is cool, dip cookies in and eat. Serves four to six. Leftover fondue can be refrigerated and used the next day as an ice-cream topping.

IN THE MICROWAVE...

Microwave the butter in a large glass measuring cup or casserole on high for 45 seconds to 1½ minutes. Stir in the sugar, cocoa and evaporated milk and cook on high for 2 to 3 minutes. Stir partway through until the sugar is dissolved and the fondue is smooth and chocolaty. Continue with steps 3 and 4. If the fondue cools off and starts to get hard when you're dunking your fruit and crackers, return it to the microwave for 20 to 30 seconds on high until it's warm and runny again.

Sweet-and-sour grapes

Grapes with sour cream??? Before you say, "No thanks!" try it. You're in for a wonderful surprise.

YOU WILL NEED

750 mL	green seedless grapes, washed and dried	3 c.
250 mL	sour cream	1 c.
50 mL	brown sugar	¼ c.
25 mL	chopped walnuts or pecans (optional)	2 tbsp.

UTENSILS

measuring cup   measuring spoons
large bowl   wooden spoon

1 In a large bowl, combine the grapes, sour cream and brown sugar. Mix well.

2 Sprinkle with chopped nuts if you like. Serves six.

Fruit soup

Fruit soup may sound odd, but it's really just a milk shake in a bowl.

YOU WILL NEED

500 mL	berries (any kind)	1 pint
125 mL	water	½ c.
15 mL	orange juice	1 tbsp.
250 mL	buttermilk	1 c.
	sugar to taste	
4	sprigs of mint (optional)	

UTENSILS

measuring cups   measuring spoons
blender   4 bowls

1 Puree the berries, water and orange juice in a blender.

2 Stir in the buttermilk and add sugar to taste.

3 Chill, if you wish, then ladle into four bowls and garnish each with a sprig of mint.

OLD AND NEW FAVORITES

Maple butter tarts

These butter tarts are formed by patting the pastry into muffin pans — a great idea for a wonderfully gooey dessert!

1 In a mixing bowl, combine the flour, 250 g (8 oz.) of butter and cream cheese. Mix until well blended and the pastry begins to form a ball. Refrigerate for 30 minutes.

2 Use a knife to divide pastry into 20 pieces. Form each piece into a small ball and press over the bottom and sides of each muffin cup.

3 Heat the oven to 425°F (220°C).

4 In a mixing bowl, beat the eggs with an eggbeater or electric mixer until light and fluffy.

5 Add the sugar, maple syrup, vinegar, vanilla and melted butter and beat until well mixed.

6 Pour the mixture into the tart shells and bake for 15 minutes.

Blueberry brown betty

Early settlers used whatever ingredients they had to make desserts. Brown betty was usually made with apples, but as you'll see, it's also terrific when made with blueberries and served hot or warm.

YOU WILL NEED

500 mL	blueberries, washed	1 pint
250 mL	rolled oats	1 c.
125 mL	all-purpose flour	½ c.
125 mL	brown sugar	½ c.
125 mL	chopped walnuts or pecans (optional)	2 tbsp.
2 mL	cinnamon	½ tsp.
1 mL	nutmeg	¼ tsp.
50 mL	soft butter	¼ c.

UTENSILS
2.0 L (8 in.) square baking pan
small, sharp knife
measuring cups
measuring spoons
medium-sized bowl

1 Heat the oven to 350°F (180°C) and lightly grease a baking pan.

2 Cover the bottom of the pan with blueberries.

3 In a medium-sized bowl, combine the rest of the ingredients and mix well.

4 Crumble this topping over the blueberries.

5 Bake for 20 minutes. Serves six.

IN THE MICROWAVE...

Use a 23 cm (9 in.) round glass baking dish. Follow the instructions for steps 2 to 4, then microwave for 6 to 8 minutes on high. Let stand for 5 to 10 minutes before serving.

For apple lovers

Apple lovers can turn blueberry brown betty into apple brown betty by substituting six medium apples, peeled, cored and sliced, for the blueberries.

Baked apples

The pioneers baked apples whole and ate them warm from the oven as a special treat. Try them with whipped cream or ice cream.

YOU WILL NEED

6	large apples	
250 mL	brown sugar	1 c.
125 mL	raisins	½ c.
50 mL	butter	¼ c.
50 mL	water	¼ c.

UTENSILS

potato peeler	spoon
measuring cups	baking pan
small bowl	large enough for 6 apples

1   Heat the oven to 375°F (190°C).

2   Peel the top one-third of each apple with a potato peeler.

3   Use the potato peeler to remove the cores from the apples. Do not cut a hole all the way through the apple: leave the bottom intact.

4   Cut horizontally through the skin around the middle of each apple to prevent it from splitting as it cooks.

5   In a small bowl, mix the brown sugar, raisins and butter. Spoon the mixture into the holes in the apples.

6   Put the stuffed apples in the baking pan, sprinkle the water around them and bake for 30 minutes. Serve hot or cold. Makes enough for six.

IN THE MICROWAVE...

Follow the instructions for steps 2 and 3, then pierce the skin in a few places with the tip of a sharp knife. Continue with step 5, then arrange the apples in a circle around the outside of a microwavable dish. Make sure to leave the center of the dish empty. Loosely cover with waxed paper and microwave on high for 8 to 10 minutes or until the apples are tender. Let stand for 5 minutes before serving.

Applesauce

This applesauce is a snap to make.
You don't even have to peel the apples.

YOU WILL NEED

6	medium apples	
1	lemon	
15 mL	apricot jam (optional)	1 tbsp.

UTENSILS

medium pot with lid	fork
grater	sieve
knife	wooden spoon
measuring spoons	medium bowl

1 Put the apples in a pot.

2 Grate the lemon and add the grated rind to the apples. Slice the lemon in half and squeeze the juice into the pot.

3 Cover the pot and cook over medium-low heat for 20 minutes or until the apples are tender when pierced with a fork.

4 Remove the pot from the heat and set aside to cool. When the apple mixture is cool, pour it through a sieve placed over a bowl. Use a wooden spoon to rub the apples against the sieve so that the applesauce goes into the bowl. The skins and seeds will not go through the sieve; throw them away when you're done.

5 Stir the jam into the applesauce. Makes about 500 mL (2 c.) of applesauce.

IN THE MICROWAVE...

Peel, core and quarter the apples, then place them in a large microwavable bowl with the juice of ½ lemon. Cover with plastic wrap and microwave on high for 4 to 6 minutes or until the apples are tender. Set aside to cool, then mash with a potato masher. Stir in the jam.

Rice pudding

This is a creamy type of rice pudding with a touch of spice. It has to be cooked on the stove for a long time — but it's worth waiting for.

YOU WILL NEED

175 mL	uncooked long-grain rice	¾ c.
1 L	milk	4 c.
500 mL	whipping cream	2 c.
250 mL	sugar	1 c.
2 mL	salt	½ tsp.
2 mL	vanilla	½ tsp.
2 mL	nutmeg	½ tsp.
5 mL	cinnamon	1 tsp.

UTENSILS
measuring cups
measuring spoons
large saucepan
wooden spoon
8 dessert dishes

1 Put the rice, milk, whipping cream, salt and half of the sugar in a large saucepan over high heat. Bring it to a boil, then reduce the heat to medium-low and cook for 1 hour or until thickened. Stir the mixture often so it doesn't burn or stick to the bottom of the pan.

2 When thickened, remove the pudding from the heat and cool to room temperature, then stir in the vanilla, nutmeg and cinnamon.

3 Spoon into 8 individual ovenproof dessert dishes or one large ovenproof bowl and sprinkle the top with the remaining sugar.

4 Turn the oven on to broil. Place the pudding under the broiler for 30 seconds or until lightly browned. Serve at room temperature or chilled. Serves eight.

Poprice?

Did you know that puffed-rice cereal is made from rice that is popped much the same way as popcorn? Hmmm … funny it's not called poprice.

Pumpkin pie with a graham-cracker crust

If you're making this pie in the fall, you can ask an adult to help you cook fresh pumpkin. Otherwise use canned pumpkin.

YOU WILL NEED

75 mL	butter	⅓ c.
375 mL	graham-cracker crumbs	1 ½ c.
50 mL	sugar	¼ c.
3	eggs	
125 mL	honey	½ c.
2 mL	ginger	½ tsp.
2 mL	nutmeg	½ tsp.
2 mL	cinnamon	½ tsp.
1 mL	salt	¼ tsp.
1 mL	allspice	¼ tsp.
1 mL	ground cloves	¼ tsp.
375 mL	cooked fresh or canned pumpkin	1 ½ c.
250 mL	evaporated milk	1 c.

UTENSILS

measuring cup	1.0 L (10 in.) pie plate
measuring spoons	wire whisk or wooden spoon
small saucepan	
mixing bowl	

1 Melt the butter in a small saucepan over a low heat.

2 In a mixing bowl, combine the crumbs and sugar.

3 Add the melted butter and stir well.

4 Press the crumb mixture into the bottom and sides of a pie plate. Chill in the refrigerator while making the filling.

5 Heat the oven to 325°F (160°C).

6 In a large mixing bowl, combine all the rest of the ingredients. Use a wire whisk or wooden spoon to mix them together well.

7 Pour the mixture into the chilled piecrust and bake for 1 hour and 20 minutes or until a knife inserted in the center comes out clean. Remove the pie from the oven and set it aside to cool. Serve warm or cold with whipped cream, if you wish. Serves eight to ten.

IN THE MICROWAVE...

To make a crust, microwave the butter for 45 seconds on high. Continue on to steps 2, 3 and 4, but use a deep 23 or 25 cm (9 or 10 in.) glass pie plate. In a large bowl, combine all the rest of the ingredients, PLUS 45 mL (3 tbsp.) of all-purpose flour. Mix with a wooden spoon and pour into the chilled piecrust. Microwave on medium for 20 to 24 minutes, until almost set in the center.

Chocolate mousse

You wouldn't find this recipe in a pioneer kitchen. It's a new old favorite.

YOU WILL NEED

500 mL	chocolate chips	2 c.
50 mL	water	¼ c.
175 mL	whipping cream	¾ c.
50 mL	sugar	¼ c.
50 mL	toasted coconut	¼ c.

UTENSILS
small saucepan
2 medium-sized bowls
measuring cups
electric mixer
spoon

1 Put the chocolate chips and water into a pot and melt them over low heat, stirring constantly. Turn off the heat and set the chocolate aside to cool.

2 Use an electric mixer to beat the whipping cream until it stands up in stiff peaks. Add sugar.

3 Slowly add the cooled melted chocolate to the whipped cream and mix them together.

4 Spoon into four dessert dishes and sprinkle with coconut. Chill for 2 hours in the refrigerator. Serves four.

MICROWAVE TIP

Instead of melting the chocolate chips and water on the stove, put them in a large glass measuring cup and microwave on medium for 4 to 6 minutes. Stir to help the chocolate melt.

Extra-fancy rice cereal squares

These no-bake squares are great when fancied up with chocolate chips and crunchy peanuts.

YOU WILL NEED

75 mL	butter	⅓ c.
750 mL	marshmallows (miniatures work best)	3 c.
75 mL	chopped nuts	⅓ c.
1 L	rice cereal	4 c.
75 mL	chocolate chips	⅓ c.

UTENSILS
2.0 L (8 in.) square cake pan
measuring cups
measuring spoons
large saucepan
wooden spoon
spatula

1 Lightly grease the cake pan.

2 Melt the butter in a large saucepan and stir in the marshmallows. Cook and stir over low heat until the marshmallows are melted.

3 Remove from the heat and stir in the chopped nuts, rice cereal and chocolate chips. Mix well.

4 Use a spatula to lightly press the mixture into a cake pan. Let cool before cutting into squares. Makes about 16 squares.

IN THE MICROWAVE...

Microwave the butter for 45 seconds to 1 minute on high. Stir in the marshmallows and microwave for 2 to 3 minutes on high. Stir occasionally to help the marshmallows melt. Continue with steps 3 and 4.

Grow a marshmallow?

Today's marshmallow is really a spongy white candy made from sugar. But the original sweet was made from the roots of the marshmallow plant.

FROSTINGS AND SAUCES

Cream cheese frosting

YOU WILL NEED

125 mL	cream cheese at room temperature	½ c.
25 mL	soft butter	2 tbsp.
250 mL	icing sugar	1 c.
2 mL	vanilla	½ tsp.

UTENSILS

mixing bowl   wooden spoon
knife

1 Put all the ingredients into a mixing bowl and mix together with a wooden spoon until smooth and creamy.

2 Use a knife to spread the frosting on the cake.

Orange glaze

YOU WILL NEED

75 mL	icing sugar	⅓ c.
75 mL	orange juice	⅓ c.

UTENSILS
small saucepan
wooden spoon

1 Put the sugar and orange juice into a small saucepan and cook, stirring, over low heat until the sugar dissolves and the glaze is hot.

IN THE MICROWAVE...

Make the orange glaze by microwaving all the ingredients in a large glass measuring cup for 45 seconds to 1½ minutes on high.

Chocolate sauce

1 Pour all of the ingredients into the top of a double boiler. (See page 8 for how to use a double boiler.)

2 Stir over medium heat until the chocolate has melted.

3 Cool the sauce to room temperature, then refrigerate until ready to use. Makes about 375 mL (1½ c.) sauce.

YOU WILL NEED

1	175 g (8 oz.) package chocolate chips	
250 mL	whipping cream	1 c.
5 mL	instant coffee (optional)	1 tsp.

UTENSILS
measuring cup
measuring spoons
double boiler
wooden spoon

IN THE MICROWAVE...

To make the chocolate sauce, combine all the ingredients in a large glass measuring cup and microwave on high for 2 to 4 minutes. Stir partway through to help melt the chocolate.

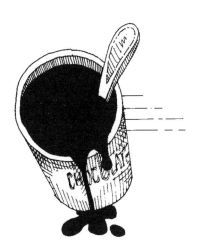

INDEX

N

Nanaimo bars 29
Nuts
    Crispy nuts 42
    Crunchy granola 43
    Maple nut pie 31
    Nutty orange balls 14
    Nutty popcorn 41
    Pistachio carrot cake 27
Nutty orange balls 14
Nutty popcorn 41

O

Oatmeal
    Crunchy granola 43
    Oatmeal sunflower crispies 12
Octobers 17
Orange bread 39
Orange glaze 61

P

Peanut butter
    Giant peanut-butter cookies 23
    Peanut-butter candy cheesecake 30
    Peanut butter and banana
      milk shake 44
Pies
    Chocolate sundae pie 32
    Fruity pizza pie 33
    Lemon angel pie 34
    Maple nut pie 31
    Pumpkin pie with a
      graham-cracker crust 57
Pistachio carrot cake 27
Popcorn
    Nutty popcorn 41
Poppy-seed banana bread 38

Puddings
    Chocolate mousse 58
    Rice pudding 56
Pumpkin pie with a
  graham-cracker crust 57

R

Real lemonade with mint 46
Rice pudding 56

S

Sweet-and-sour grapes 51

T

Tarts
    Maple butter tarts 52
Tomato soup cake 26
Tropical fruit shake 46